Noel Gallagher's
High-Flying Words

Noel Gallagher's
High-Flying Words

Compiled by Melissa Bond

\B^b\
Biteback Publishing

First published in Great Britain in 2015 by
Biteback Publishing Ltd
Westminster Tower
3 Albert Embankment
London SE1 7SP
Copyright in the selection © Melissa Bond 2015

Melissa Bond has asserted her right under the Copyright, Designs and Patents Act 1988 to be identified as the author of this work.

All rights reserved. No part of this publication may be reproduced, stored in a retrieval system or transmitted, in any form or by any means, without the publisher's prior permission in writing.

This book is sold subject to the condition that it shall not, by way of trade or otherwise, be lent, resold, hired out or otherwise circulated without the publisher's prior consent in any form of binding or cover other than that in which it is published and without a similar condition, including this condition, being imposed on the subsequent purchaser.

Every reasonable effort has been made to trace copyright holders of material reproduced in this book, but if any have been inadvertently overlooked the publishers would be glad to hear from them.

ISBN 978-1-84954-959-2

10 9 8 7 6 5 4 3 2 1

A CIP catalogue record for this book is available from the British Library.

Set in Helvetica

Printed and bound in Great Britain by
CPI Group (UK) Ltd, Croydon CR0 4YY

Contents

Introduction..vii
Biography...xi
Trivia...xxi

Brotherly love...1
Musical appreciation.....................................15
Oasis...41
Literary criticism..51
Songwriting...59
The rock 'n' roll lifestyle................................73
Journalism..83
Family ties..89
The X Factor...97
The big issues..103
Personal musings..117

Introduction

Just over twenty years ago, Britpop pioneers Oasis changed the face of the UK music scene forever with the release of *Definitely Maybe* – an album that went seven times platinum and has sold more than 10 million copies to date. As the driving force behind the band – and, more recently, his own High Flying Birds – Noel Gallagher has been hailed as one of the finest songwriters and most notable rock stars of his generation.

Off stage, however, the forthright frontman is just as notorious for his quick wit and unfettered remarks as he is for his musical genius and iconic songbook. From stories of his infamously tempestuous relationship with younger brother Liam to candid appraisals of the (lesser) talents of fellow musicians, the Mancunian motormouth's readiness to speak his mind and ask the big questions – seriously, what *is* a wonderwall? – have ensured he remains the most charismatic, sincere and refreshing figure in the music industry today.

Never one to shy away from controversy, Noel has spent more than two decades commenting on topics as diverse as politics and popstars, novels and narcotics, fame and family, the Beatles and Blur – as well as the not infrequent blowing of his own trumpet – leaving a trail of public reaction in his wake. Undeterred, Noel continues to commend and offend in equal measure, and it is hoped this compendium of his sharpest insights and most gratuitous insults will prove a handy and entertaining guide to the tell-it-like-it-is musings, sage bon mots and classic high-flying words of Mr Noel Gallagher.

Biography

Noel Thomas David Gallagher was born on 29 May 1967 in Manchester. The son of Irish parents, Peggy and Tommy Gallagher, he was the couple's second child after his brother Paul. Noel's birth was followed five years later by that of his younger brother Liam.

Due to an unhappy childhood, during which the boys suffered domestic abuse at the hands of their alcoholic father, Noel developed a stammer, and was described by Liam as 'the weirdo of the family'. Despite the eventual separation of his parents, Noel continued to be a troubled child and developed into a rebellious adolescent. Aged thirteen, he was sentenced to six months' probation for shoplifting (although it was during this period that he began to teach himself to play guitar), and he was regularly caught truanting. Two years later, he was expelled from school for throwing a bag of flour over a teacher.

Having maintained limited, if uneasy, contact with their father, the teenage Gallagher brothers secured jobs at Tommy's building company. Noel moved out of his family home in 1988 to live with his then girlfriend Louise Jones, with whom he would enjoy an on-again-off-again relationship for several years. When the couple split for good in 1994, he stated, 'I don't think I'll ever get over it.'

Noel continued to work in construction until he sustained an injury that forced him into recuperation – though this gave him the time he needed to hone his guitar-playing and song-writing skills. (He claims to have written at least three of the songs on *Definitely Maybe* in this period.) However, by the late 1980s, Noel's musical talents were overshadowed by his unemployment and recreational drug use.

After auditioning unsuccessfully to be the new vocalist for Mancunian rock outfit Inspiral Carpets, Noel took a job as the band's roadie, touring with them for two formative years. Upon his return home in 1991, he discovered brother Liam had become the frontman of a local band, The Rain. Noel was distinctly unimpressed. Rejecting Liam's offer to become their manager, Noel instead agreed to join the band – but only on the condition that they let him have complete creative control. According to one source, Noel told the band (newly renamed Oasis): 'Let me write your songs and I'll take you to superstardom.'

In 1993, Oasis journeyed to Glasgow to perform at a talent-scouting gig. Their four-song set caught the attention of the founder of Creation

Records, Alan McGee, who took their demo tape to Sony America and invited the band to meet with him in London the following week. They would go on to sign a six-album contract, and tour with The Verve as the opening act.

Oasis's first single 'Supersonic', penned by Noel, reached No. 31 in the UK charts in early 1994, but it was the release of the band's first album that propelled them to success. *Definitely Maybe* became the fastest-selling debut album in British history at the time, entering the charts at No. 1. This was followed the subsequent year by their first No. 1 single, 'Some Might Say', and another chart-topping album, *(What's the Story) Morning Glory?*, which became the second fastest-selling album ever in the UK.

With this newfound fame and fortune came the rock 'n' roll lifestyle, which both Noel and Liam embraced wholeheartedly. The Gallaghers became notorious for their drinking, fighting, drug abuse, extravagant spending and celebrity friends (including Paul Weller, Mick

Jagger, Johnny Depp and Kate Moss), and were featured regularly in the tabloids. Tensions between Noel and Liam also began to intensify – leading, at one point, to a physical fight with a cricket bat – and the brothers' persistent altercations would prove to be the band's eventual undoing.

Oasis went on to have even greater success with the release of, arguably, their two most famous singles, 'Wonderwall' and 'Don't Look Back in Anger', which charted at No. 1 and No. 2, respectively. As the decade progressed, Oasis became associated with the Britpop movement, alongside rival group Blur. Antagonism between the bands began to swell, culminating in their defining head-to-head chart battle in 1995, dubbed 'The Battle of Britpop', which would pit the release of Oasis's 'Roll With It' against Blur's 'Country House'. When Blur came out on top, Noel expressed a wish for the victorious Damon Albarn and Alex James 'to catch AIDS and die' – a comment he quickly apologised for following public outcry. The feud continued, however, with the Gallagher brothers singing a brief rendition of Blur's hit 'Parklife' at the Brit Awards the following year, with Liam changing the key lyric to 'Shitelife'.

Despite playing two sold-out gigs at Knebworth in 1996 to around a quarter of a million fans, the band's third album, *Be Here Now*, released the following year, failed to live up to the expectations created by its predecessors, leading to a media backlash against Noel and the band. (He later blamed the problems with the album on his drug-addicted state at the time of its creation.) Shortly after, Noel faced further criticism for attending Tony Blair's high-profile 'Cool Britannia' party at 10 Downing Street. A photograph of Noel sipping champagne with the newly elected Prime Minister conflicted with his supposed 'working-class hero' image, prompting Damon Albarn (who had declined his invitation to the event, as had Liam) to comment: 'Enjoy the schmooze, comrade.'

That same year, Noel married fellow '90s wild child Meg Matthews, who gave birth to their daughter, Anaïs, in 2000. They divorced the subsequent year on the grounds of Noel's alleged infidelity, although he later claimed his affair was fabricated in order to speed up the separation process.

In 1999, Oasis's rhythm guitarist Paul 'Bonehead' Arthurs quit the band, although his departure did little to worry Noel ('It's hardly Paul McCartney leaving the Beatles, is it?'). Despite this reshuffle of the line-up and Noel's continued in-fighting with Liam, the success of Oasis carried them well into the new millennium, and, in 2007, the band collected an Outstanding Contribution to Music Award at the Brits. By this point, Noel was in a relationship with publicist Sara MacDonald, and the couple would go on to have two sons together, Donovan and Sonny.

However, Noel's issues with his brother were also coming to a head, and, in August 2009,

Noel announced he was leaving Oasis, stating he 'simply could not go on working with Liam a day longer'.

Following the band's well-publicised break-up, Noel moved on to other projects, notably the formation of Noel Gallagher's High Flying Birds in 2011, whose eponymous debut album was met with generally positive reviews. Noel also got married to long-term girlfriend Sara the same year.

During his career, Noel has become known for his outspoken and often controversial comments – a trait that prompted music mogul Simon Cowell to offer him a spot on *The X Factor*'s judging panel, which Noel, perhaps unsurprisingly, declined. He also garnered attention when he criticised the selection of Jay Z as Glastonbury headliner: 'I'm not having hip-hop at Glastonbury. It's wrong.' In response to Noel's comments, Jay Z opened his set at the festival with a cover of 'Wonderwall'.

Noel Gallagher's High Flying Birds released their second album in 2015, and have confirmed plans for a third.

Noel and Liam have yet to reconcile.

Trivia

- Despite being a talented songwriter, Noel is dyslexic and cannot read or write music.
- Noel's pets include two stray cats he adopted, Benson and Hedges – named after his favourite brand of cigarettes.
- Noel is a lifelong Manchester City FC fan, and confessed to 'crying like a baby' when they won the Premier League title.
- Noel made the decision to quit drugs in 1998, after admitting he could 'hardly remember a thing' about the previous five years of his life.
- Despite being naturally left-handed, Noel plays the guitar with his right hand.
- As a child, Noel's nickname was Brezhnev – after the former Russian President who was known for his bushy eyebrows.
- At Noel's wedding to wife Sara, comedian Russell Brand was his best man.
- Noel chose the moniker High Flying Birds as an homage to Jefferson Airplane's song 'High Flying Bird'.
- Noel is believed to have an estimated net worth of $60 million.

Brotherly love

"It's hard working with members of your own family. Especially if one of them's Liam Gallagher."

"I read these interviews with him and I don't know who the guy is who's in these interviews – he seems really cool – because the guy I've been in a band with for the last eighteen years is a fucking knobhead."

"Sure, I love Liam. But not as much as I love Pot Noodle."

"Liam has only two problems: everything he fucking says and everything he fucking does."

"His fans come up to him after shows and I hear him giving all this gobshite, and I think, 'Shut up, you twat, I babysat for you!'"

"He's rude, arrogant, intimidating and lazy – the angriest man you'll ever meet. He's like a man with a fork in a world of soup."

"He's the man who put the 'tit' in 'attitude.'"

Interviewer: "Do you [and Liam] still have physical fights?"

Noel: "No. The last time was in March or May, and we haven't done since…"

Interviewer: "Who won?"

Noel: "I did. He claims it's because he was drunk, but I claimed [it was] because I had a cricket bat in my hand."

"Maybe he did get cast in the role of the performing fucking monkey by the press, and maybe I got cast as the man behind the curtain. Maybe he wanted to be the Wizard of Oz instead of the monkey."

Meg (Noel's first wife): "There's a little boy at the door who wants an autograph."

Noel: "Is it Liam again?"

Noel: "Explain the word 'compromise' to me in a sentence. You haven't got a clue!"

Liam: "It means, like … 'backing up.'"

Noel: "That's 'reverse.'"

"[Liam's] gone to the zoo. Seriously. The monkeys are bringing their kids to go have a look at him."

Interviewer: "If you could dedicate one song, any song in the world, to Liam, what song would you choose?"

Noel: "Do you know the nursery rhyme 'The Wheels on the Bus Go Round and Round'? That one."

Interviewer: "Why?"

Noel: "I think he would enjoy it."

"You know, like, when you go to someone's house, and in their fridge they've got, like, a bottle of champagne in the fridge, and it's got, like, a fork or a spoon in it to keep it fresh? Well, [Liam] came to my house once, opened the fridge and said: 'Why is there a fork inside that champagne bottle?' And I said: 'Well, if you put a fork inside, it keeps it fresh.' About two days later, I went round to his – and he had a fork inside a bottle of milk."

"First time we played live, Liam sang 'sun-shee-ine' during 'Cigarettes and Alcohol' – he hated the way he sung it. Now we can't stop him: 'Fancy a pee-int down the pub?'"

"Liam puts lager before music, bless him."

"My argument is: 'Be a cunt all you want, but let's do the gig first.' His argument is: 'I'm just being a dick all the time.' Repeat endlessly until fucking 2009."

"I like to think I keep it real. Liam keeps it surreal. And somewhere between the two we get on alright."

"Problem is: I can't fire him because my mum would kill me."

"I always get this: 'Excuse me, mate, are you Liam Gallagher?' Fuck's sake. Sometimes, even when they ask me, I say no, and they're like, 'You don't half look like him!'"

"I say I hate Liam all the time. But I never mean it."

"He's an idiot, but he's my idiot."

Musical appreciation

On U2

"Play 'One'. Shut the fuck up about Africa."

On the Kaiser Chiefs

"I did drugs for eighteen years and I never got so bad as to say: 'You know what? I think the Kaiser Chiefs are brilliant.'"

On Keane

"People say I seem very negative about new music. Well, if somebody asks me what I think of Keane, I'll tell them I don't like them. I'll obviously take it a step too far and grossly insult the keyboard player's mam or something, but I'm afraid that's just me."

"I feel sorry for Keane: no matter how hard they try, they'll always be squares. Even if one of them started injecting heroin into his cock, people would go, 'Yeah, but your dad was a vicar, goodnight.'"

"Traditionally speaking, the three biggest twats in any band are the singer, the keyboardist and the drummer. I don't need to say anything else."

On the Arctic Monkeys

"I would rather drink petrol straight from the nozzle at a garage than listen to an interview with Alex Turner from the Arctic Monkeys. I mean, wouldn't you?"

On Beyoncé

"If artistry is shaking your ass on stage, she's fucking great."

On Lady Gaga

"It's all about the meat suit and the controversy … but where's the fucking music?"

On David Guetta

"Surely David Guetta is the biggest con that's ever been pulled in all of music? I've seen him at festivals and there are 70,000 people stood watching him play his own CD. Idiots."

On Madonna and her exercise regime

"Do you want to get so supple that you can eventually stick your own head up your arse?"

On Kylie

"Kylie Minogue is just a demonic little idiot, as far as I'm concerned. She gets cool dance producers to work with her for some bizarre reason, I don't know why. She doesn't even have a good name. It's a stupid name – Kylie – I just don't get it."

On learning Westlife had beaten Oasis in the album chart

"There is no God."

On '90s pop

"I don't get the Britney thing. I certainly don't get the 'NSync, the Robbie Williams or the Gorillaz thing. There's a lot of things I don't get."

On the Scissor Sisters

"It's music for squares, man. They're huge in England, but there's no accounting for bad taste as far as the English are concerned."

On Paul Weller

"People think he's some deep god, but he's a moany old bastard. He's Victor Meldrew with a suntan."

On members of Take That

"Take That's Howard Donald said in a documentary that he hears voices at night willing him to fail. To fail at what? You don't do anything, Howard."

"Can you imagine walking through the Priory and seeing Robbie Williams coming over in a dressing gown? That's enough to drive you to heroin."

"What has [Robbie] done to me? Nothing. He's just somebody I'd like to hang."

"Robbie's still officially on strike, isn't he? From being brilliant."

On Mark Ronson

"He wants to write his own tunes instead of ruining everyone else's."

On Ed Sheeran

"You hear that kind of polished pop and then there's a ginger guy with a fucking guitar."

On Blur

"Damon Albarn is a fucking knobber. And his guitarist – who I thought was alright – seems to think that he's some intelligent super-human being. The fucking idiot. I never met the drummer, and the bassist – who I first didn't like and thought was a cunt – turned out to be quite alright. But I don't like the music, and I don't like the singer."

"That cunt is like, 'Is there a bandwagon passing? Park it outside my house.' He'll be in a heavy metal band next year when it's fashionable."

"People say we're the Rolling Stones and Blur are the Beatles. But we're the Stones *and* the Beatles. They're the fucking Monkees."

"I worked on building sites; that fundamentally makes my soul purer than theirs."

"I hate that Alex and Damon. I hope they catch AIDS and die."

On Radiohead

"Thom Yorke sat at a piano singing 'This is fucked up' for half an hour. We all know that, Mr Yorke … Who wants to sing the news? No matter how much you sit there twiddling, going, 'We're all doomed,' at the end of the day, people will always want to hear you play 'Creep'. Get over it."

"They've sold 30 million albums and they're still fucking miserable."

"Won't you fucking give it a rest, you bunch of moaning children?"

On One Direction

"Fucking idiots. They're all winning. No one's losing! The only people who are losing are idiots like me at 9.30 in the morning when you're trying to get the kids out the door for school, and they're fucking murdering one of Blondie's songs."

"Bless 'em, bless 'em. But fuck 'em at the same time."

On Mumford & Sons

"A lot of people hate them in England. I think it's the waistcoat and facial hair."

On solo artists

"[They're] generally totally insane. Elton John? Slightly eccentric. George Michael? He's mad as custard."

On Phil Collins

"Phil Collins knows he can't say anything about me because I'm the fucking bollocks, and that's the thing that does his head in. And the fact that he's bald."

"Why did he sell so many records in the '80s? I mean, fucking hell."

"Vote Labour. If you don't and the Tories get in, Phil Collins is threatening to come back from Switzerland and live here – and none of us want that."

"Just because you sell lots of records, it doesn't mean you're any good. Look at Phil Collins…"

On Paul McCartney's longevity

"Paul McCartney – one of the best songwriters of all time – has only produced manure for the past twenty-five years."

"I think he's just going senile, isn't he?"

On George Harrison describing Oasis as 'a passing fad'

"George was always the 'quiet Beatle'. Maybe he should keep that up."

"If I were in the Beatles, I'd be a good George Harrison."

On wanting to be John Lennon

"With every song that I write, I compare it to the Beatles. The thing is they got there before me. If I'd been born at the same time as John Lennon, I'd have been up there."

"I'm not like John Lennon, who thought he was the Great Almighty. I just think I'm John Lennon."

On his brother wanting to be John Lennon…

"He did once say that to me. In my mam's front room. He was talking in a Scouse accent for three days. He told me I should refer to him as 'John', and I was like, 'I just prefer "cunt", man.'"

…more than once

"He told me he thought a cold chill had touched him in Yoko's apartment. I put it to him it was the fucking air-conditioning. Yoko's getting on a bit now; she probably has it set on minus 16."

On streaming music

Interviewer: "Some people have taken their music off Spotify. Taylor Swift, for example…"

Noel: "How is the world gonna survive that? Do we know?"

"Apple Music, world radio – is that some sort of George Orwell shit going on? Unless there's a fucking section that says 'Noel Gallagher's music collection' then I won't be listening to it."

Musical appreciation

On Pop Idol

"I just want to know, what were those fuckers hoping to achieve out of this? What was that twat Dr Fox – and those other cunts – doing? Did they really think they'd find the new Elvis? They've made a mockery of singing, of selling a million records. Will Young is in *The Guinness Book of Records*, for fuck's sake! But so what? So is a bloke who jumps off the Eiffel Tower and lands in a fucking teacup. Did he write 'Strawberry Fields Forever'? No. So fuck off."

On the charts

"Chart positions are for people with manbags who get to work at 11 a.m. because they've been at a 'digital meeting.'"

"The charts are only relevant when you're top of them."

Oasis

On their success

"We are the biggest band in Britain of all time, ever. The funny thing is that fucking mouthing-off three years ago about how we were gonna be the biggest band in the world … we actually went and done it."

"We're not arrogant, we just believe we're the best band in the world."

On their old music videos

"If you needed four guys to walk around in slow motion, we were the best at that."

"A guy actually said to me on this video shoot, 'Can we do that bit again, but can you do it with a bit more energy in your eyes?' I still have no idea what he meant by that to this day. I don't know. Do you want me fucking to stare at you like a fucking serial killer?"

On continuing to play their songs

"I'm not going to cut off my nose to spite my face by saying I will never play those songs again. Nobody helped me write those songs. I'm not cheating on anybody. If I feel like playing 'She's Electric', then I'll fucking play it."

On sound bites

"Oasis can't be summed up in one word, but I could do a sentence: 'Boys from council estate made it very, very big.'"

On resolving conflict

"As bad as things get in Oasis, there's always this sibling thing that draws us back together. Or my mum gets involved."

On their biggest-selling single

"'Wonderwall': that's virtually every bird between the ages of thirty and thirty-six's favourite fucking song."

"Jay Z doing 'Wonderwall'? It was pretty funny…"

"I don't much like 'Wonderwall.'"

On being sued by Coca-Cola

"We only drink Pepsi now."

On the possibility of a reunion

"As long as everybody is still alive and still has their hair, it's always a possibility. But only for the money."

On the rest of the band (bar Liam)

"There's no point in interviewing them: they've got fuck all to say for themselves anyway."

Literary criticism

On the book trade

"People who write and read and review books are fucking putting themselves a tiny little bit above the rest of us who fucking make records and write pathetic little songs for a living … I don't get it. Booksellers, book readers, book writers, book owners – fuck all of them."

On literary misnomers

"My missus will come in with a book and it will be titled – and there's a lot of these, you can substitute any word, it's like a Rubik's Cube of shit titles – *The Incontinence of Elephants*. And I'll say, 'What's that book about?' And she'll say, 'Oh, it's about a girl and this load of fucking nutters…' Right, so it's not about elephants, then? Why the fuck is it called *The Incontinence of Elephants*? Another one: *The Tales of the Clumsy Beekeeper*. What's that about? 'Oh, it's about the French Revolution…' Right, fuck off. If you're writing a book about a child who's locked in a fucking cupboard during the fucking Second World War … he's never seen an elephant, never mind a fucking giraffe."

On celebrity autobiographies

"Why is Posh Beckham writing a fucking book of her memoirs? She can't even chew chewing gum and walk in a fucking straight line at the same time, let alone write a book."

On Shakespeare

"[I was watching Jude Law in *Hamlet* – it was] four hours long, and there wasn't one single minute that I knew what was going on. I was thinking, 'I know they're speaking English but it's just all fucking gibberish.' I can appreciate the acting and the way they learned all those lines but … what the fuck was going on?"

On fiction

"I mean, novels are just a waste of fucking time. I can't suspend belief in reality … I just end up thinking, 'This isn't fucking true.'"

Literary criticism

Songwriting

Noel: "I regret going to the Caribbean island of Mustique with Mick Jagger, Jerry Hall, Johnny Depp and Kate Moss and trying to write [third album] *Be Here Now*."

Interviewer: "Didn't Sir Mick step in and offer any sage advice?"

Noel: "No, he was spending too much time trying to get off with Kate Moss to be arsed."

"If you're given a blank cheque to record an album and as much studio time as you want, you're hardly gonna be focused. There's a pub round the corner and Kentucky Fried Chicken – you just get lazy."

"Sally does not exist. There is no Sally. It just fit the lyrics … I've never met a girl called Sally in my entire life."

"What's a wonderwall? Who cares? It sounds great."

"I put drug references in Oasis songs because I take them – I write about what I know."

"I got this tape from America that had apparently been burgled from the Dakota Hotel ... [John] Lennon was starting to record his memoirs on tape. He's going on about 'trying to start a revolution from my bed, because they said the brains I had went to my head'. Thank you, I'll take that."

Noel: "Liam wrote nine songs for the new album, and three of them were amazing."

Interviewer: "And the rest were…?"

Noel: "Utter shite."

"I write the first line and the end word. 'Supersonic' – it's like, 'Well, what rhymes with that?' And you start off with 'a', and you go, 'Atomic, bionic…' Then you go, 'Gin and tonic! Alright, that'll do.' It's no big deal. You just write it down and people go, 'Wow! Feeling supersonic … give me gin and tonic. Wow!' Basically because it rhymes."

"I'd like to thank Dylan and Lennon and McCartney and Townshend and Morrissey and Marr. And all those other people I've been robbing for the past twenty years."

"If you listen [to Green Day's 'Boulevard of Broken Dreams'], you'll find it is exactly the same arrangement as 'Wonderwall' … They should have the decency to wait until I'm dead. I at least pay the people I steal from that courtesy."

"Someone told me 'Supersonic' was about teenage prostitution. Shit. It's about a 9-stone Rottweiler called Elsa who was in the studio where we were recording."

"If I wrote songs about my own life, they would be more boring than James Blunt – if that's at all possible, which, we all know, it's not."

"All I ever wanted to do was make a record. Here's what you do: you pick up your guitar; you rip a few people's tunes off; you swap them round a bit; you get your brother in the band (punch his head in every now and again) – and it sells. I'm a lucky bastard."

"You can't really write a full album about your missus: she'll start getting the wrong idea and thinking you like her."

"I was always open to other people writing in this band, but no cunt ever did."

"Most of the songs I write are under the influence of one thing or another."

Interviewer: "Man, you've written some great songs."

Noel: "Indeed."

The rock 'n' roll lifestyle

On 'the look'

Interviewer: "You're probably one of the most down-to-earth rock stars I know … but you do wear shades when the sun's not shining."

Noel: "Well, it's in the manual, isn't it? It actually says in the rock-star book: 'Thou shalt wear shades at all times, preferably indoors.'"

On extravagant purchases

"Liam got a Rolex. I got a Rolls-Royce. Which is brilliant, because I can't drive and Liam can't tell the time."

"When you first get your royalties, you do stupid things with money. I do own a pair of Elvis's headphones. I bought them from Sotheby's, and I don't know what I was expecting to hear – maybe a voice saying, 'Fangyew very much.' And then you realise they're just a pair of crappy old headphones."

On crazy fans

"Americans are crazy. They have this fascination with throwing their shoes on stage. I've been to a lot of shows in me life, some good and some bad, but I was never moved to take off me shoe and throw it at the lead singer."

"Next year I hope to get a stalker or two, because I don't believe you've arrived until you get a stalker."

On having a role model

"We've all been there: we've all thought we were Paul Weller at some point. Even Paul Weller thought he was Paul Weller at some point."

On trashing hotels

"Until you've actually thrown a television set out of a window you don't even know the sense of joy that brings."

"We used to proper fucking wreck things, it was total destruction. But we've grown up now – it's just mild trashing."

On the downside of fame

"I bought a really nice jacket in Japan, and in this big, massive swirl of people, someone with a pen scribbles on my jacket. It's fucking ruined."

"I absolutely loved being famous – it was all great … Up until the point when it wasn't."

On 'healthy' rock stars

"I've seen seeds in Coldplay's dressing room. Fucking seeds! Where's the parrot?"

"What the fuck is Morrissey going on about? Does he really not like meat? He must like sausages. Everybody likes fucking sausages."

On retail therapy

"I stand in the queue at Waitrose. More rock stars should do that. Forget therapy, go to the supermarket and interact. The staff in my local Waitrose are really blasé about me now. They'll be like, 'Him? Oh, he's in here all the fucking time. And, between me and you, he doesn't eat very well.'"

On living life to the full

"What's problematic about playing stadiums and driving around in private jets and drinking champagne at eight o'clock in the morning? What's wrong with that?"

"This guy came up to me from some band and he said: 'Man, I'd hate to be you right now – no privacy at all.' And I was thinking: 'Sure thing, man. I have a fucking Rolls-Royce, $1 million in the bank, a fucking mansion and my own jet, and you think you feel sorry for me? What are you? I'd hate to be you – broke as hell, living on the dole.'"

Journalism

"If you see an *NME* journalist at any of the gigs – and, let's face it, they're pretty easy to spot, they don't stray far from hospitality, wear God-awful clothes, particularly the shoes, got dreadful hair and that kind of 'mug me' look about them – give 'em a clip round the earhole from me and tell 'em to behave."

"There's a real journalistic way of going: 'Well, Liam would always want to be Noel because he's the talent and he writes the songs, and Noel would always want to be Liam because he shags all the supermodels.'"

"I keep getting told this by journalists. [They] say to me, 'You seem so happy.' I go, 'No, it's the Prozac.'"

"What would you rather read? 'The guy from Keane's been to a rabbit sanctuary because one of the rabbits needed a kidney implant so he swapped his with it', or 'Liam Gallagher sets fire to a policeman in cocaine madness while his brother Noel runs down Oxford Street nude'?"

Family ties

On being a good father

"I don't want to blow my own trumpet here, but I have got a few mugs that say 'Best Dad in the World'. They wouldn't buy them for no reason, would they?"

On attempting to move to LA with his wife

"We was getting the paperwork done to transfer all our worldly goods over there, and then *she* went and got pregnant. I've still not got to the bottom of how that fucking happened."

On educating his children

"My kids go to private school because I don't want them coming home talking like Ali G."

On raising a daughter

"She'll text me, 'Who are the Stone Roses?' And I'll say, 'Ahh, OK. Well, the Stone Roses were the second-best band to ever come out of Manchester.'"

"I wouldn't have expected her to be into anything other than One Direction when she was twelve, [but] if she's into One Direction when she's twenty-two, she's getting shunned."

On raising a son

"My son ain't going to be miserable: he's going to be the child of a rock star. The end."

"My son actually said to me once, 'You should get your hair cut like Gary Barlow.' I've shunned him since. He now lives in the shed."

Family ties

On his pet cat

"Well, I didn't name him. Let's get that straight. My four-year-old named him Boots. Not after the chemist, obviously, although if he'd named him Superdrug, that would've been fucking brilliant."

On making his mother proud

"As soon as we go home, she sits us down at the kitchen table. She tells us we swear too much and says: 'So what's this about you sprinkling cocaine on your Corn Flakes, Noel? And Liam, is this true about you going to whore houses?' There's nothing we can say."

"Mum, if you're watching: there were no prostitutes – just traditional drugs."

Family ties

The X Factor

"If they'd asked me to do one show, I might have done it, just so I could put everybody through – every midget, dwarf, obese fuckwit, the lot – to the next round: 'You've all got the fucking X factor!' But they wanted me for the full series, and I was like, 'You mean I'd have them coming round my house?' No way. I'd have people crying on my couch while I'm telling them, 'It's been the toughest decision I've ever had to make – the Knebworth set list was nothing on this – but you're in my final four! Now go and mow my lawn, you fat cunt.'"

"There's a boy band with eight lads in it. You cannot get eight people to sing in tune, live. It is impossible. If the Beach Boys couldn't do it, no one's doing it. And there they are: miming their little hearts out to a Snow Patrol cover. Honestly, I have a vein in the side of my neck that jumps out about 4 inches."

"*X Factor* winners last for about six months, then they end up in rehab. That's very interesting to see: some fucking fat idiot works in a supermarket, convinces himself that he's a fucking superstar – but has he got any songs? Not really. When he finally realises that, actually, he's a fucking fat idiot from a supermarket who got lucky, he turns to alcoholism and ends up killing his own gerbils. That's brilliant. But the music's shocking."

"It's kind of about who's got the biggest sob story this year, you know? 'Oh, my fucking cat died and its outstretched paw was pointing at the letter "x" on the pools coupon, so now I've come here today, Simon, to sing "What's New Pussycat?"' Come on, do us a favour: get a proper job."

The big issues

On religion

"The Word of God is in the Bible, right? And in the Bible, it doesn't mention dinosaurs – so that [can't] be [the] truth. Because if God created the humans first, where did the fuckin' dinosaurs come from?!"

On charity concerts

"I'm not sure about this Live 8 thing. Correct me if I am wrong, but are they hoping that one of these guys from the G8 is on a quick fifteen-minute break at Gleneagles and sees Annie Lennox singing 'Sweet Dreams' and thinks, 'Fuck me, she might have a point there, you know'? It's not going to fucking happen, is it? Keane doing 'Somewhere Only We Know', and some Japanese businessman going, 'Aww, look at him! We should really fucking drop that debt, you know.' It's not going to happen, is it?"

"You can't put a load of rock stars on stage and expect to wipe out global poverty. That's ludicrous."

On extraterrestrial life

"If I saw an alien, I'd tell it to fuck right off because, whatever planet he came from, they wouldn't have the Beatles or any decent fucking music … I ain't going nowhere with them."

On justice reforms

"My laws would be: smoke where you want; drink what you want, whenever you want; get the age of consent down; legalise drugs; kill all the people who like grunge music; kill all surfboarders; melt the snow; anybody who wears a cowboy hat should get the electric chair."

On politics

"I don't have a crystal ball; I didn't see [Tony Blair] was going to turn into a cunt. I was thirty, off me head on drugs, and everyone was telling me we were the greatest band since who knows. Then the Prime Minister invites you round for a glass of wine – it all becomes part of the high. Why not? I thought it would give me mum a laugh. I didn't go thinking, 'I endorse this government's policies in every respect.' I went to have a look at the curtains."

On the monarchy

"I wouldn't wish the royal family dead … just seriously maimed. I'd take a couple of legs off."

On space travel

"If I ever get to go to the moon, I'll probably just stand on the moon and go: 'Hmmm, yeah, fair enough. Gotta go home now.'"

On the economy

"I know there's a world financial crisis going on, but I went for a Chinese the other night in Oslo, right, and guess what? No fortune cookie! What the fuck is all that about? How is anyone supposed to plan for future events pertaining to one's personal situation if you don't know what the future holds?"

On current affairs

"These fledging democracies in the Middle East – they're actually fighting for their freedom. And what are they rioting for in England? Leisurewear."

"There's nothing good in the news. You're not telling me CNN is all cats in trees, are you? Nothing can be good if Piers Morgan is in it, you know what I mean?"

On Princess Diana's death

"Half the people wouldn't visit their grandmother's grave … then they go and throw flowers at the coffin of some bird they've never met."

On technology

"I thought [the] internet was something that fishermen use."

On food wastage

"If you're going to buy a doughnut, eat the fucking doughnut. Don't have a bite and then chuck it on the floor. Eat the fucking doughnut!"

On the nuances of language

"Progression is going forwards. Going backwards is regression. Going sideways is just gression."

On the environment

"You can't blame rock stars for global warming when the Chinese, the Indians and the Americans have been pumping out shit into the atmosphere for the last hundred years."

On illegal substances

"Didn't go into rehab like all me mates did – fucking lightweights."

"If there were gold medals for taking drugs for England, then I'd have won a shitload! I did enjoy it, but it kind of got to the point where I'd done them all and that was it. There was none left, and I just thought, 'Can't be arsed any more.'"

"I stopped taking drugs because I was talking about aliens, pyramids, the Beatles and who shot JFK a bit too much."

Personal musings

On being opinionated

"People think [I'm] controversial for the answers [I] give to silly questions in interviews, but if somebody asks me what I think about Live 8 or Robbie Williams or Madonna, I'm not thinking about insulting those people; I say what I genuinely feel is in my heart. My conscience is clean, d'you know what I mean? Y'know, I'm true to myself – fuck everybody else."

On his intellect

"I'm equal part genius, equal part buffoon."

On his image

"Don't lay a finger on me eyebrows, or I'll sue you, fuckers."

"I'm not fat and bald – I'm doing alright."

On his childhood

"I couldn't be bothered doing my fuckin' homework, so I just sat there playing one string on this acoustic guitar. I thought I was really good for about a year until someone tuned it up. Then I thought, 'I can't play the fuckin' thing at all now. I'm gonna have to start all over again.'"

On winning awards

"It is hard to be modest at times like these, so I won't even try … You are all shite!"

"It doesn't make me feel any more special than I do every day."

On the prospect of a knighthood

"I won't get offered it: I can't see many ex-glue-sniffers among the medals, can you?"

On social media

"Nobody needs to know what colour socks I'm wearing – black, by the way – I don't need to be on Facebook. I've got six friends, and I'm trying to get rid of one of those so I can count them all on one hand."

On bending the truth

"I came up with the greatest excuse one day – it was actually my crowning moment as a liar. I used to spend a lot of time in my bedroom playing guitar. I went to the shops for Mum and I came back and she'd found a bag of hash in my sock drawer – a big block of draw. So she says, 'I've just found this upstairs.' And, right off the top of my head, I went, 'Ah, well, you see, what that's for is wiping the strings on my guitar.' I said, 'Violin players use it.' And she said, 'Oh, really?' And I went, 'Yeah, look' – I got my guitar and rubbed all my strings with pot – 'it makes them sound better.' And she went, 'It does sound better!' And I went upstairs and thought, 'You're a fucking genius!'"

On his career

"If you could sum up my career with films, Oasis was a cross between *The Wolf of Wall Street* and *Saving Private Ryan*."

On the red carpet

"I was walking along the red carpet and all I could hear were people shouting what I thought was, 'Liam, Liam!' I thought, 'The idiots have got the wrong brother…' I turned around and said, 'Oi! I'm not Liam, I'm Noel!' I wondered, 'How could they get that wrong?' But then I realised they were actually shouting, 'Leo!' It turns out that Leonardo DiCaprio was right behind me…"

On paying audiences

"We've not got respect for any crowd, not even our own ... I look at it this way: £32.50 is nowhere near enough money to come and see me play guitar. It should be £32.50 for each member of the band, it's that fucking good!"

On one-upmanship

Noel: "I'm only 5ft 8."

Interviewer: "I'm 6ft 1."

Noel: "Good for you. I'm a multimillionaire."

On naming his band

"I don't know if I'm going to keep that name or not. Probably will: it's such a fucking good name. I might change the 'Noel Gallagher' bit … Call it Paul McCartney's High Flying Birds and see if I sell any more tickets in America."

Interviewer: "Noel Gallagher's High Flying Birds – how did you come up with that?"

Noel: "I'm a fucking genius."

On missing a gig

"Apologies again to the people of Mexico City who didn't get to see a show on Monday when I selfishly decided to sit on a toilet for six hours and shit out the entire contents of my being through the eye of a needle and puke what was left into a wastepaper bucket … at the same time! So very sorry I chose to get ill."

On self-improvement

"I don't have the genetic make-up of a frontman – but I'm learning how to do it."

On smoking

"When I met [my wife], she smoked Marlboro Lights and I smoked Benson & Hedges, and she made me change to Marlboro Lights because she reckons Bensons were bad for me. And then, do you know what she did? She gave up smoking. So now I smoke birds' fags and she's the picture of health."

On coming to London

"I thought Big Ben was going to be massive. I was underwhelmed."

On proving yourself

"Be good, don't be outrageous. Anybody can be outrageous. I could go to the *Rolling Stone* office and fucking shit on top of a boiled egg, right? And people would go, 'Wow, that's fucking outrageous!' But is it any good? No, because, essentially, it's just a shit on top of a boiled egg."

On being an animal-lover

"Is there anything funnier than a dog going down the high street with his face hangin' out the window? Y'know, when you see dogs in the passenger seat, someone's wound down the window, and the dog's got his face out the window and he's like, 'Woah! We're goin' 43 miles an hour!' And he's got his tongue out! The second funniest thing is dogs in hats! Is there anything funnier than a dog wearing a hat on holiday? Is there anything funnier than a dog in sunglasses? I don't think so. I don't think so."

On getting on with the neighbours

"Ewan McGregor was my neightbour, right, and he came round my house the night he got the part of Obi-Wan Kenobi. I just happened to have two of those lightsaber toys, so I said, 'Come on, in the back garden.' And we had a fucking lightsaber fight."

On gift ideas

"I don't want a monkey … I want a fucking aeroplane."

On the dating life of Russell Brand

"At least I'm not shagging Geri Halliwell. I mean, fucking hell – out of all the Spice Girls – not Ginger!"

"I go to him, 'Just have one fucking beer. One beer!' And he says to me that if he has one beer he'll probably end up in a crack house in King's Cross within forty minutes. I'm like, 'Brilliant, I'll come with you.'"

On footballer Zlatan Ibrahimović

"This guy is a fucking idiot. I do not like him. He is full of crap. He is like my brother: he talks a lot but can't back it up; cool tattoos and a big mouth."

On humility

"All the people down here who have cited me as an influence: you are fucking welcome."

"I am the master of the universe. Goodnight."

Interviewer: "So who is the most influential artist of the past twenty-five years?"

Noel: "What a fucking silly question. I'm fucking sat right here."

On shopping

"I went into this shop and picked out a load of records. I had a spectacular hangover, but was in there for over an hour. These records were in fucking great nick – all vinyl – so I put them on the counter and the bloke said, 'Can I have your name, please?' So I said it was Noel. And then he asked me for my last name, and I said, 'Gallagher'. He punched it into the computer, and I thought, 'This is a bit fucking fascist!' Then he told me my name wasn't coming up on the computer, and I said, 'Why would my fucking name be coming up on your computer?' Then he said, 'Because this is a library…' I left all the records at the counter and went back to the pub – where I should have stayed in the first place."

On his funeral

"I'm not really bothered because I won't be there. I don't give a shit."

On a final note

"If you tell me now that the record-buying era is over, that makes me sad that the culture of buying and believing in a record is over. That era is over and the belief is that music is for hire and for rent – the money that you pay lets you access everybody's music but own none of it – I think that's a sad day. I understand that it's the future, but it's a sad day."